CW00864360

Lesson 1

of the Magical Order of the Atlantic Oracle:

Vivid thinking

Grand Master .-. Ma

Bibliografische Information der Deutschen Nationalbibliothek:

Die Deutsche Nationalbibliothek verzeichnet diese Publikation in der Deutschen Nationalbibliografie; detaillierte bibliografische Daten sind im Internet über http://dnb.dnb.de abrufbar.

Herstellung und Verlag: BoD –
Books on Demand, Norderstedt

ISBN: 978-3-7504-9812-9

Introduction

By using this book, you accept this disclaimer in full.

No advice

The book contains information. The information is not advice and should not be treated as such.

No representations or warranties

To the maximum extent permitted by applicable law and subject to section below, we exclude all representations, warranties, undertakings and guarantees relating to the book.

Without prejudice to the generality of the foregoing paragraph, we do not represent, warrant, undertake or guarantee:

- that the information in the book is correct, accurate, complete or non-misleading.

- that the use of the guidance in the book will lead to any particular outcome or result.

Limitations and exclusions of liability

The limitations and exclusions of liability set out in this section and elsewhere in this disclaimer: are subject to section 6 below; and govern all liabilities arising under the disclaimer or in relation to the book, including liabilities arising in contract, in tort (including negligence) and for breach of statutory duty.

We will not be liable to you in respect of any losses arising out of any event or events beyond our reasonable control.

We will not be liable to you in respect of any business losses, including without limitation loss of or damage to profits, income, revenue, use, production, anticipated savings, business, contracts, commercial opportunities or goodwill.

We will not be liable to you in respect of any loss or corruption of any data, database or software.

We will not be liable to you in respect of any special, indirect or consequential loss or damage.

Exceptions

Nothing in this disclaimer shall: limit or exclude our liability for death or personal injury resulting from negligence; limit or exclude our liability for fraud or fraudulent misrepresentation; limit any of our liabilities in any way that is not permitted under applicable law; or exclude any of our liabilities that may not be excluded under applicable law.

Severability

If a section of this disclaimer is determined by any court or other competent authority to be unlawful and/or unenforceable, the other sections of this disclaimer continue in effect.

If any unlawful and/or unenforceable section would be lawful or enforceable if part of it were deleted, that part will be deemed to be deleted, and the rest of the section will continue in effect.

Law and jurisdiction

This disclaimer will be governed by and construed in accordance with Swiss law, and any disputes relating to this disclaimer will be subject to the exclusive jurisdiction of the courts of Switzerland.

Inhaltsverzeichnis

Introduction

Dear seekers of wisdom,

Now that the predicted five thousand years have passed since the great masters revived the holy order of the Atlantic oracle, it is our duty to fulfil the prophecy and to pass the ancient knowledge of the Atlantic oracle on to the world.

We, the last three grand masters, are aware of this responsibility. That is why we decided to pass on the secret knowledge with the instruction for special rituals. These rituals allow a true seeker to acquire the knowledge through self-knowledge. To those that only read the instructions, the gate will remain closed. Only those who implement them will find the secret treasure.

To acquire the wisdom, that lies within the holy teachings, it is essential that you approach them step by step without skipping only the smallest one. That is how the adepts of the order have been doing it for thousands of years.

Pay attention to the correct order of the teaching letters and do not get this order confused. Otherwise, you will go astray and take the risk of losing many things in life.

Those who follow the path of the order with a pure heart, will grow as persons and become pure vessels for magical knowledge, which the order has preserved for mankind for thousands of years and which it will now pass on to human kind. He will acquire the maturity and the strength that is necessary *for the order to find him and take him in.*

But be careful. There are many imposters and unworthy that occur on behalf of the order to enrich themselves. To resist their lies is one part of the test, which will only be passed by the truly worthy.

The grand master of the golden feather

GM .-. Ma
in the year 5000 of the order

The order has been equally run by all masters. Even female adepts are of course welcome. The usage of male grammatical forms only serves the purpose of easier readability.

Instruction of thinking properly

In the subsequent teaching letter we will deal with the question of which power thinking properly can have and why it should be explained at the beginning of every instruction.

Thoughts are powers

Thoughts may be perceived as fleeting by laymen because they appear in a great number and come and go at any moment. There seems to be no possibility of controlling them, we feel at their mercy.

The initiate, however, recognizes thoughts as powers that are trying to manifest themselves within ourselves. We can decide which thoughts we want to admit and *therefore give power and thus grant them to influence our existence. Thoughts become material reality; they are just like light, warmth or electricity. Those who know how to understand them, are able to see them and those who are sensitive can even feel them.*

Thoughts have been proven as physical processes with the help of technical measures for quite a long time. We can even organize them according to their kind. But modern technologies and our thoughts are also connected in a different way: As we think while working on a machine, we move things and communicate. Think of cranes that are navigated by humans or think of telephones. Without our thoughts nothing would move. Those who, however, achieved master ship can even do this without technical devices.

We send our thoughts out into the world, which is constantly connected with all of us as their creators by a spiritual bond. Those thoughts seek to unite with other thoughts and to manifest themselves as mightier powers.

If we send out thoughts of sadness, anxiety or fear, the thoughts will find other thoughts of the same kind and reflect on us with the new regained strengths. The same applies to our thoughts getting strength from our confidence, joy and courage. However, these powers do not just reflect on the person who sent them, but they also influence his environment and the environment of those whose thoughts connected with the first person's thought.

If we do not want to be at the mercy of

our thoughts, we have to start to dominate our way of thinking. The domination over our thoughts is the first task that every adept hast to master before he can take the next step of the magical instruction. If he does not master it, he will only experience no or only bad and unwanted results.

Constant practice is the only thing that enables the true adept to accomplish things that are generally considered to be impossible.

Just because we know of this barrier, that separates those who are truly seeking from those that are just curious, we can disclose the knowledge of the order. Only the one who grew with the hard work and became mature, will be able to use the knowledge. Everyone else will not get wiser with this exercise. For those it will be the same as reading a children's story.

Intensifying of the positive thoughts

When thoughts grow in reality and eventually reflect on us, it is obvious that we need to think well and positively. The more intense and clearer we are able to do this, the more success we will have. The adept has to use all of his strength and concentration to adopt an intense and positive way of thinking.

However, all external impressions prevent him from fully concentrating on this task and from learning this ability which is fundamental to his development. Not only the adept, but every person of every rank has to constantly test whether or not he is still master of his head because who does not have the control over his thoughts, is dominated by them.

Only those who want to change something with their thoughts have to learn how to think intensively. For this, he needs to discipline his thoughts in that way that he is able to ignore, push away or suppress every other thought, image and idea as well as all disturbing external influences. Neither eyes, ears and hands nor nose and tongue may distract him. In short: No obstructive idea or sensation is allowed to creep in.

The master becomes one with his thoughts. They fill him in completely. There is no place left inside him that is not pervaded by his thought. Or rather: He is the thought. Both his own physical reality and his environment do not exist anymore during the period of exercise. Only his spiritual »self« is still alive, filled with his most powerful thought. To achieve this, the seeker needs to bundle the roving thoughts and focus on a goal.

Bundling of thoughts

One can show that thoughts – if they are determinedly controlled – are able to have an effect on the material reality. For this, one has to look closely at a part of his body for a long time. All other thoughts have to be excluded; one focuses the entire thinking on this spot. If you succeed in staying concentrated blood will gather at the spot and there will be a slight reddening after some time.

From history of science many examples are known where people could alleviate or even cure diseases and malformations with the help of focusing their thoughts on that. The famous American psychologist and therapist Milton Erickson reports of one example:

1919, shortly after graduating from high school, Erickson contracted polio and fell into coma. Initially, it seemed as if he would not survive the disease. After three days, however, he regained consciousness, but was fully paralyzed. Unable to move he sat in a rocking chair. The intense desire to look out of the window is said to have lead to a slight movement of the rocking chair. This ideomotor experience motivated him to continue practicing. With the help of his imagination he worked on making his paralyzed muscles function again. After almost a year he was able to walk on crutches and attended the university of Wisconsin. Contrary to the advise to rest he was given by doctors, he went on a 1200 miles long canoe trip on Mississippi river. Because of this he regained considerable physical strength. Two *years after that he was able to walk without crutches, he merely limped with his right leg.*[1]

Such a focus is not magic, but a simple scientific and physical reality, that only appears to be magic to the eyes of an uninitiated and inexperienced. On the other hand, the bundling of thoughts is the basis for magic which has to be mastered in order to continue the training. The exercise may also serve those who are not adepts, for example if they want to increase their health and well-being.

Further uses of such concentration techniques are known from Indian gurus and fakirs. For example, they could make a grain germinate within a short time with the help of the power of thought.

---

[1] Source: http://de.wikipedia.org/wiki/Milton_H._Erickson

The exercises

Magic is based on discipline and exercise. That should be clear to anyone, because how should someone that does not know how to master one self, master high arts? In order to facilitate the first steps, it is best to create a suitable environment. We do this by arranging an enclosed space so that neither street noise nor any other external influences can enter.

We have to remove or at least shut off everything that could distract us. This applies to telephones, televisions and computers. Ideally, there should be no pictures or other decoration. It makes it easier for someone without practice to concentrate on the task. However, the room should not be completely empty. It is important that you have a bed or a sofa in this room because in some exercises you will have to stretch out your body to completely relax your muscles.

Always choose the same time period for the exercises. The early morning or the late evening are ideal. It is important that you are always undisturbed and awake at the time you chose (seven days a week). Those who are still half asleep or completely exhausted will not achieve the desired results. Also make sure that you are not disturbed by family members, friends or neighbors during the exercise.

Those who have no room that they can use for the exercises, should at least establish an area within the room in which one can practice quietly. Once you have achieved a certain amount of exercise, you will be able to disconnect your senses from external *impressions solely through your willpower, anyway. After that you will be able to exercise successfully even during the biggest disturbance.*

Exercises of the first stage: Controlling your muscles

After the external conditions are set, it is now important to get ready yourself. For that you have to get rid of physical restlessness. As it is impossible to calm a ship on a stormy ocean, it is also impossible to concentrate within a restless body.

Many people have the habit of instinctively giving in to an external stimulus. If they hear a sound from somewhere or see a shadow, the immediately turn their heads to the source of the sound or shadow. Others cannot sit still without tapping with their foot, playing with their fingers or pulling on their clothes and body. All of those movements distract, especially beginners.

To practice resting your body, sit down

somewhere in public where there is a lot of traffic, noise and disturbance. Keep your feet parallel to each other on the ground and put your legs parallel as well. Now, place your hands on your thighs with your palms facing downwards and look at the ground in front of you. Force yourself to be in absolute peace and focus on a chosen spot.

At the beginning you will not succeed for a long time, maybe for two or five minutes. Repeat this exercise daily and extend the duration by five minutes every day. If you practice this ritual daily, you will soon be able to sit still for a whole hour. Do not let yourself get discouraged by failures. Failures show us on what we still have to work. Those who give up will not achieve this first goal. But those who keep up the practice and who work on themselves, will soon succeed – and this applies to all of the exercises of this teaching letter.

Another aspect of external discipline is regularity. This routine represents the second foundation for inner concentration. Make it a habit to begin with your exercises at the same time every day. Start at the exact same minute. Only with the powers of discipline and habit you will achieve real mastership.

The third exercise of controlling your body is about coming to a rest when externally everything is calm. Especially when the environment is calm and quiet some people start to continually play with their hands. To break this habit, place your hands on the edge of the table and stretch your thumbs downwards along the edge of the table. You could do this exercise while reading *an interesting book which lies on the table.*

Exercises of the second stage: Controlling your thoughts

Once you have achieved external discipline and put your body to a rest, you are ready to venture controlling your thoughts. This is the key that opens the door to all the other powers. Every mental phenomenon is based on the power of thoughts. Whether it is telepathy, sending out a breath for medical purposes, influencing matter with the help of willpower, clairvoyance, clairaudience or those arts that only the most experienced masters exert: all of them are based on the control over thoughts. That is why the adept is supposed to focus on acquiring this ability and also the members of the order of the other ranks have to constantly work on their spiritual discipline because they know of the dangers that they will otherwise evoke.

Especially the adept that is still at the begging of his path, has to keep in mind to perform the following exercises carefully and that he does not lose his touch until he is able to concentrate his thought on one spot.

Other abilities of similar importance are going to be taught in the following teaching letters. The same seriousness is necessary for those.

Once the adept has steadied himself with the help of the exercises of the first stage, he is ready for practicing the concentration of thoughts. Let us take an experience of your life as a basis for the first exercise of the second stage: Select a journey that you have made in your life; neither the destination nor the company or the occasion are crucial. However, if you choose a journey that you retrospectively perceive as pleasant and that you can remember well, the exercise will be more motivating and easier.

The journey

Sit down every day at a certain time in the room that you chose for the exercises and close your eyes and ears in an enjoyable manner. Position yourself comfortably, but make sure that it is not comfortable enough to fall asleep. The exercise involves intense concentration. Now you begin to think about the selected journey.

Imagine yourself making the same journey again. Think about how you prepared the trip, how you dressed appropriately and how you packed everything you needed. Then you left the house and got into your car – or did you walk to the next bus stop? Which people did you walk into? And how did you interact with them?

The more intensively you can imagine everything, the more details you will remember. You will feel the wheels rolling on the roadway, the temperature ...

Experience the whole journey again with all senses and take your time. The exercise is not about getting it over as quickly as possible, but to awaken all of your sensory impressions, your thoughts and your feelings, that you had during the journey. Dwell upon your spiritual journey until your alarm clock indicates that the time you predetermined for the exercise has run out.

Beware, however, of your thoughts wandering. Especially the novice may find it difficult when his thoughts do not wander further naturally. Almost automatically he will start to develop new ideas and make new plans.

Once a strange thought shows up that does not belong to the journey, you should dispel it. This also includes thoughts such as: »What would be if I had done X instead of Y?« or »What would Z have done?« In short: Everything, that did not really happen during your journey has to be rejected.

It may be that the exercise will not be successful at first. Do not let yourself get discouraged. Repeat the journey once day. For this you always have to choose the same journey and start at the beginning.

For one, you will be amazed at how much you will remember. With every practice you will remember more details, things that you thought you had long forgotten. On the other side, you train and discipline your mind with it. What is most important about the exercise is that because of the repetition, your thoughts will become more vivid and real.

This exercise should take about 20 to 30 minutes daily. If you want to, you can increase the duration a bit. More important than the duration, however, is the depth and the vividness of the impressions and thoughts.

Only when you manage to think through the journey without distraction for several days, you are ready for the next exercise.

Items of the first stage

For the second exercise of this group you have to select a small, simple item that you have on hand. This could be a knife, a key or a *lamp.*

Consider the item closely. Capture its shape, its color and its weight. Think about its purpose and about the material that it is made of. Also consider how the item is made. This is not a scientific analysis. If you do not know how it is manufactured, you can speculate. However, your mind must not run off track. All the thoughts that are not linked to the item are forbidden. If your thoughts wander off, discipline them.

Schedule about five minutes for the exercise on the first day. If you were successful, gradually increase the duration by further five minutes until you have reached 20 minutes. If you have finished your chain of thoughts, start all over again until the time has expired. If you find concentrating difficult, you can whisper your thoughts at the beginning. The external stimulus may help you to stay in the »here and now«. But do not use this technique more than three to four times. If you do it without help, drop the whispering.

Change the item after one week. You should go from complicated to simple objects. It is way more complicated to concentrate on a pin for a certain amount of time than to concentrate on a complex figure.

If you have completed the exercise with four to five items, you can move on to the next exercise.

Items of the second stage

For this exercise you have to pick up the

item again. This time we will go from the simple to the complicated items. Let us start, for example, with the mentioned needle, a pen or a button.

Consider the selected item for a longer time. After that close your eyes and keep the exact mental image that you have made in your mind. When you open your eyes again, compare your mental image to the item and recognize the differences.

Close your eyes again and correct the image until every detail matches the original. Check and correct until everything corresponds with each other.

Practice this exercise until you can even accurately imagine the most complicated item with closed eyes after some minutes of concentrated examining. Every exercise should last no longer than 30 minutes. If it does not work with one object, go back to an easier one and increase the level of difficulty after you were able to successfully reproduce the easier object.

The mental reproduction is not solely about the image. You should rather learn to think vividly. Your thoughts have to include mental seeing, feeling, sensing and sometimes even smelling or tasting. This is the only way to make an intense stimulation possible.

What does that exactly mean? If we for example go back to the needle, then it is not enough to see the tip of the needle. You rather have to perceive the danger of pricking yourself with the needle, that point of the needle that could pierce into your flesh.

If you imagine a cut lemon, it is not enough to perceive its form, its color, the pores on its surface, the flesh of the fruit, the smell, the taste and its weight. Your imagination of the acid of the fruit has to be so vivid that you feel how your saliva flow is stimulated, how the acid travels through your mouth.

Only those who are used to thinking in this vivid way, will be put into the place of learning how to specifically manifest his thoughts.

Once you have passed this exercise successfully, you have laid the foundation to moving forward to more difficult tasks.

Exercises of the third stage: More abstract exercises of thoughts

Now imagine an object, without having a model, and, similar to the earlier exercise, start thinking about the purpose, the material and manufacturing of the object. Start with the more complicated items and go on to the easier ones in this exercise.

If you were successful with the exercise with the objects, you have to work with individual animals (e.g. pets) or persons in the same way. If you can do this as well, jump from one item to the other. This is about guiding your full attention from one item to another at command. Consider an object for two to three minutes and then switch to the second one and after that back to the first one. Now you continue with your chain of thoughts from where it was interrupted.

It is therefore about guiding a chain of thought artificially and later finding back to it. This change is to be carried out for four to five times, but not longer than half an hour straight.

The goal is to find back to clear, vivid imaginations after switching thoughts.

Those who have passed every of the earlier introduced exercises successfully, will from now on practice them with open ears and expose themselves deliberately to external noise. You can, for example, practice the exercises in busy parks or in a sidewalk cafe. In this way, the adept will learn to withdraw himself from the external world and to concentrate his mind completely on one thing.

Exercises of the fourth stage: The mind

Sit down with a book anywhere outside, in a park or in a restaurant, where you feel comfortable. Now pick up the book. Read a passage that you find interesting or that you like. Afterwards, write down what you have read from memory.

The more you are able to concentrate yourself, the more accurate will be what you have written down. At the beginning there might only be a summary of what you have read on the piece of paper. With some practice and concentration your transcript will become more accurate.

We will go from easy to difficult in this exercise again. We will begin with short texts, that interest us and that excite our curiosity.

With increasing training, the adept will choose topics that he is not familiar with and that he is not too interested in. The musical person will maybe start with a book about art and will finish with a legal text.

Begin with shorter texts of about 20-40 lines and gradually increase the amount until you work with whole essays. It should not be worked for more than half an hour straight. It is better to practice several times a day for 20 minutes.

Even complex examples of calculation (of course, solved mentally) are helpful for learning high concentration. Another exercise is reverse thinking. In this example, the alphabet is recited backwards (from Z to A) or one recites the major keys according to the amount of #-signs, the periodic table or something similar.

Everyday areas of exercising

Our exercises of thoughts are not confined to meditation in a quiet room. It is the task of the adept to always be interested in his environment and to perceive it.

Regardless of whether you perceive a person, a beautiful building, a bug at the side of a way or a vehicle: Memorize everything and practice at home to liven up what you have perceived in your mind. Especially the ability to remember people this way and to imagine them vividly is important for the last group of exercises.

Exercises of the fifth stage: The vivid image of people

Take a picture of an acquainted, living personality and withdraw yourself into your exercise room. Put the image on the seat in front of you. It is best to choose two similar chairs. Sit down on one of the chairs and position the picture on the other one. Alternatively, you can hang the image up on a wall at eye level.

Concentrate on the photograph. With increasing concentration, you will come so far that you will only perceive the image. Now, apply your ability of vivid thinking. In your thoughts let the person become bigger and let the person rise from the picture. The photograph will fade into the background until it disappears completely. Only the vividly imagined person will stand in front of you as a physical image.

Repeat the exercise as often as possible within 30 minutes. Good results require many repetitions and thus opportunities for more practice.

When the image manifests itself realistically in your mind, try to get into rapport with the other person. For this you have to talk to the imaginary phenomenon. Pay attention to the thoughts that arise during this process. After much practice you will get in touch with the person on the picture.

When making this mental contact, make sure to do it at a time when you can be sure that the person you are talking to is asleep. This way the contact will become easier and otherwise the other person could be harmed.

Those who accomplished this exercise, can perform the same procedure without having a picture of the person. For this he firstly has to project the photograph of the person from his mind onto the chair and then he can fill it in vividly.

Performing the exercises

The individual exercises build up on each other. Accordingly, one is not advised to go on to the next exercise as long as the previous one has not been mastered. Moreover, »passed« exercises are not supposed to be left alone. A clever adept repeats them over and over. If one exercise does not work, it should be repeated. Only when one really mastered the exercise, one can go on to practicing the next exercise.